Made in the USA
Columbia, SC
25 November 2023

27083572R00057